FULL COURT PRESS
Basketball Skills and Drills

RACHEL STUCKEY

CRABTREE
Publishing Company
www.crabtreebooks.com

Author
Rachel Stuckey

Editors
Marcia Abramson, Kelly Spence

Proofreader
Wendy Scavuzzo

Photo research
Melissa McClellan

Design
T.J. Choleva

Cover Design
Samara Parent

Prepress Technician
Tammy McGarr

Production coordinator
Margaret Amy Salter

Developed and produced for
Crabtree Publishing by BlueApple*Works* Inc.

Consultant
Greg Verner, President
Ontario Basketball

Photographs
Cover: Thinkstock

Interior: © Andy Cruz: title page middle right, p 11 top right, 13 left, 14, 15, 16, 19, 30 top; 123RF: © rook76 (p 18 left, 21 left); Bigstock: © Pavel Shchegolev (p 9 top); © EricBVD (p 11 bottom); © Monkey Business Images (p 29 top right); © robeo (p 29 bottom); Shutterstock.com: © Eric Broder Van Dyke (title page) © Africa Studio (basketball behind page numbers; © Torsak Thammachote (TOC); © Danny Smythe TOC bottom; © Dewitt (texture background); © Brocreative (page top left); © Eugene Sergeev (page top border); © prophoto14 (page bottom border); © Slavoljub Pantelic (Slam Dunk photo); © Doug James (p 4); © Stephane Bidouze (p 5 left); © Aspen Photo (p 6, 7 top right, 7 bottom right, 12 bottom, 20 left, 23 top, 25 top, 28–29 top); © Richard Paul Kane (p 8, 12 left); © grafvision (p 10); © Ivica Drusany (p 12 top); © Photo Works (p 12 right, 27 right); © Vedran Vidovic (p 19 middle); © Dziurek (p 19 right); © Faraways (p 20–21 top, 20–21 bottom); © Monkey Business Images (title page middle left, p 21 right, 24); © Maxisport (p 22); Keystone Press: © Ed Suba Jr (p 13 right); © Meunier / Icon Sports (p 23 bottom); © Joe Rimkus, Jr (p 27 left); Thinkstock: © nickp37 (p 11 left); © Jupiterimages (p 30 bottom); Public Domain: U.S. Air Force Photo / Staff Sgt. Devon Suits (p 5 right); Library of Congress: p 18 right, 26 left; Creative Commons: El Pantera (p 6–7 top); Michael Barera (p 6 bottom); El Coleccionista de Instantes (p 7 bottom); Keith Allison (p 9 left, 17, 25 bottom); chiuchiu11 (p 26 right); David Holt (p 28 bottom)

Library and Archives Canada Cataloguing in Publication

Stuckey, Rachel, author
    Full court press : basketball skills and drills / Rachel Stuckey.

(Basketball source)
Includes index.
Issued in print and electronic formats.
ISBN 978-0-7787-1536-8 (bound).--
ISBN 978-0-7787-1557-3 (paperback).--
ISBN 978-1-4271-7754-4 (pdf).--ISBN 978-1-4271-7750-6 (html)

    1. Basketball--Juvenile literature. 2. Basketball--Rules--Juvenile
literature. 3. Basketball--Equipment and supplies--Juvenile literature.
I. Title.

GV885.1.S78 2015   j796.323   C2015-903198-2
                                            C2015-903199-0

Library of Congress Cataloging-in-Publication Data

Stuckey, Rachel.
  Full court press : basketball skills and drills / Rachel Stuckey.
      pages cm. -- (Basketball source)
  Includes index.
  ISBN 978-0-7787-1536-8 (reinforced library binding : alk. paper) --
ISBN 978-0-7787-1557-3 (pbk. : alk. paper) --
ISBN 978-1-4271-7754-4 (electronic pdf) --
ISBN 978-1-4271-7750-6 (electronic html)
  1. Basketball--Juvenile literature. I. Title.
  GV885.1.S88 2016
  796.323'2--dc23
                                            2015022910

Crabtree Publishing Company

Printed in Canada / 082015 / BF20150630

www.crabtreebooks.com   1-800-387-7650

Published in Canada
Crabtree Publishing
616 Welland Ave.
St. Catharines, ON
L2M 5V6

Published in the United States
Crabtree Publishing
PMB 59051
350 Fifth Avenue, 59th Floor
New York, New York 10118

Published in the United Kingdom
Crabtree Publishing
Maritime House
Basin Road North, Hove
BN41 1WR

Published in Australia
Crabtree Publishing
3 Charles Street
Coburg North
VIC 3058

CONTENTS

Basketball Around the World   4

How to Play   6

The Rules of the Game   8

Warming Up   10

Ball Handling   12

Passing the Ball   14

Shooting the Ball   16

Rebounding   18

Playing Defense   20

Great Guards   22

Fantastic Forwards   24

Amazing Centers   26

Sportsmanship   28

Play Like a Pro   30

Learning More   31

Glossary and Index   32

TAKE IT TO THE NET!

BASKETBALL AROUND THE WORLD

Basketball is a fast game with a short history! Basketball was invented in 1891 by James Naismith at a YMCA in Massachusetts. The sport was soon played all over North America by men and women. By the 1920s, there were leagues and touring teams, as well as international competitions. In 1932, eight countries formed the International Basketball Federation. Basketball became an Olympic sport in 1936, just 45 years after it was invented!

BASKETBALL LEAGUES IN NORTH AMERICA

The National Basketball Association (NBA) is the top men's professional league in North America. The league was formed in 1949 when the Basketball Association of America (BAA) and the National Basketball League (NBL) joined forces. The new NBA held its first game in Toronto, Ontario. The Women's National Basketball Association (WNBA) began in 1997. Men and women can also play in smaller professional leagues in North America. There are professional leagues in more than 70 countries around the world.

More fans are watching WNBA games on TV than Major League Soccer!

4

ON THE PLAYGROUND

There are many forms of basketball. Half-court games are very popular because they allow people to play with fewer people and in a smaller space. Half-court basketball is usually played in playgrounds and backyards. Opponents score points by shooting at the same basket. Players can practice their shooting skills on a half court with playground games based on basketball such as 21, Around the World, and HORSE.

Even in small and poor communities, kids can play basketball as long they have a ball and a hoop. This game was played in El Nido, Philippines.

BASKETBALL ON WHEELS

Wheelchair basketball is a very competitive and popular variation of basketball. The sport is played in the Summer Paralympic Games. Wheelchair basketball was created by wounded World War II soldiers. The game is played on a regular basketball court and follows the same rules. Only minor changes had to be made for the wheelchairs. The sport is so popular that some countries have mixed teams that include non-disabled athletes who use wheelchairs only to play the sport.

All you need to play basketball is a basket and a ball. The NBA and WNBA use a court that is 94 feet (28.7 m) by 50 feet (15.2 m). The court is divided in half by a midcourt line and each basket has an area in front of it called the **key**. There is a large semi-circle around each basket and key called the three-point line. The basket rim or hoop is 18 inches (46 cm) across the middle and is attached to a backboard. The basket's rim must be exactly 10 feet (3 m) from the ground. Basketballs are made of hard rubber filled with air. A size 7 basketball is 29.5 inches (75 cm) around. Women and youth play with a size 6 ball, which is 28.5 inches (72 cm) around.

Two companies, Spalding and Wilson, make many of the basketballs used in North America. Wilson supplies the NCAA tournament, while the NBA and WNBA use Spalding balls.

Backboard

Sideline

Three-point line

Midcourt line

Free Throw Line

College and high school courts are slightly different than pro courts.

JUMPING FOR THE BALL

Basketball is played by two teams of five players who score points by shooting the ball into the other team's basket. The game begins at the center of the court. The referee throws the ball in the air and two opposing players jump up to gain control of the ball. This is called the **jump ball**.

GOING FOR THE NET

Teams **dribble** and pass the ball until a player is free to shoot the ball at the basket. The opposing team tries to block the shots and steal the ball. Basketball is a fast game—the ball is always moving and players have to hustle to keep up.

*The jump ball at the start of a game is also called the opening tip or **tip-off**.*

Basketball players wear a uniform of shorts and a shirt. Many players also wear high-top shoes to help protect their ankles from injuries.

THE RULES OF THE GAME

The team that controls the ball is on **offense** and the other team is on **defense**. Once a team has **possession** of the ball, they shoot the ball within a certain amount of time on the **shot clock**. Basketball is divided into quarters and halves. Halfway through the game, the teams switch sides of the court and aim for the other basket. A regular basket is worth two points, a basket shot from the three-point line is worth three.

MOVING THE BALL

Players can only move the ball by passing it to another teammate, or by dribbling it as they run. Players may not walk or run while holding the ball. This is called **traveling**. The **three-second rule** limits the amount of time players can be in the key without the

ball. When a ball goes outside the lines, it is **out-of-bounds**. The team that last touched the ball loses possession, and the other team gets to throw the ball in from the out-of-bounds line.

When a referee calls out-of-bounds, the clock stops. A designated player throws the ball back in, and the clock restarts when another player touches the ball on the floor.

A FOUL

When a player interferes illegally with another player, it is called a **foul**. Most fouls are committed by players on defense, but offensive fouls are possible, too. When players are fouled, they may get to take one, two, or three **free throws**, which are worth one point each. Other players cannot interfere with free throws. If players commit too many fouls, they must leave the game.

Players line up on either side during a free throw.

THE REF

Referees make sure players follow the rules. They blow their whistle when rules are broken, stopping the game clock. Along with fouls, refs call **violations** such as traveling which result in loss of the ball. Referees must be very fast to keep up with the players. Other basketball officials include scorekeepers and timekeepers.

Referees use hand signals to indicate violations and fouls.

WARMING UP

It is important to warm up your muscles before doing any physical activity. Playing sports when your muscles are cold can cause injury. Making sure your muscles are loose and warm will keep you strong and ready to play b-ball.

DYNAMIC WARMUP

Start warming up with a short jog around the gym or playground, or by skipping rope for five to ten minutes. When your body is warm, you can begin a **dynamic warmup** that keeps you moving and loosens up your muscles. Doing stretches when your body is cold can lead to injury. Basketball teams often do warmups together before practice and games. But you should take time to warm up even on the playground. Leg swings, walking lunges, running high knees, back pedals, vertical jumps, and arm swings are some good dynamic exercises for basketball players.

Dynamic stretches are an effective method for warming up for most sports.

WARMING UP WITH THE BALL

Basketball teams always warm up with shooting and ball handling skills before a game. There are different types of drills that allow players to practice many skills at once. Team drills involve passing, taking shots, moving around the court in an organized way, and taking turns working with the ball. It's important to warm up by shooting the ball from different positions on the court, including taking free throws and doing lay-ups.

Players practice passes and shooting to get loose and comfortable before a game.

THE SHOOTAROUND

On game day, basketball teams often have a **shootaround**. A shootaround is an informal practice in which players take shots on the net from different positions on the court. They **rebound** each other's shots and practice different moves together. Coaches don't run drills during a shootaround the way they would in a regular practice.

The shootaround was first introduced to help players calm down game-day nerves.

BALL HANDLING

Shooting baskets may score points, but handling the ball is the most important skill in basketball. Dribbling is the controlled bouncing of the ball with your hand. When you dribble a basketball, you are pushing it toward the ground, not tapping or patting it. It is against the rules to cup the ball from the bottom—this is called **carrying**.

DRIBBLING THROUGH THE COURT

Players must be able to dribble well with both hands and keep the ball as close to the ground as possible. It's also important to dribble without looking at the ball. Players must keep their eyes on the basket and their teammates and opponents—not on the ball!

*The best players always have an eye on the ball and the flow of the game. They keep their heads up and use a firm, short dribble called a **control dribble**.*

DRIBBLING DRILL: CROSSOVER

Begin by dribbling the ball with your strong hand. Dribble the ball from your strong hand to your other hand, keeping the ball below knee level. Practice doing this while moving in a zigzag line. Start slowly, then try to speed it up. Crossover dribbling is an important skill for keeping the ball away from a defender.

Keep your eyes on the ball when starting to learn dribbling techniques. Once you get better, you'll learn how to focus on a game.

*As a point guard, Irving is the **floor leader** for his team. He was MVP of the NBA All-Star Game in 2014.*

KYRIE IRVING IS IN CONTROL

Kyrie Irving joined the NBA in 2011 and plays for the Cleveland Cavaliers. He's one of the best ball handlers in the game. He dribbles the ball between his legs and around his back with ease. His moves wow his fans, but Irving's goal is to keep his dribbling simple. Every move he makes on the court is in response to a move from his defender—he's not showing off. Irving's spectacular skills come from years and years of practice.

PASSING THE BALL

Basketball is a team sport and passing is the key to success. Players on offense pass the ball to teammates who are open. Passing the ball to a player who then makes a basket is called an **assist**. There are three main types of passes.

CHEST PASS

The chest pass is the most common. Hold the ball with two hands at chest level, then throw it to your teammate by pushing the ball forward with a quick snap. The receiving player catches the ball at chest level with both hands. Chest passes should be quick so defenders don't have time to stop the ball.

Chest passes are powerful as well as accurate, because passers can put their full weight into the throw.

SLAM DUNK!

Earvin "Magic" Johnson played for the Los Angeles Lakers for 13 years. He was known for fancy moves such as "no-look" or blind passes. He could pass the ball to teammates without looking at them, confusing his opponents and impressing the crowd. That's how he got his nickname—he was a basketball magician.

BOUNCE PASS

In a bounce pass, you push the ball toward the ground so that it bounces up toward the receiving player. Bounce passes take longer, but let you pass around defenders or under their reach. It takes practice to get the right force and angle to make a bounce pass work.

A bounce pass can be made with one or two hands. Players often use a bounce pass when a defender gets in the way of their target.

OVERHEAD PASS

The overhead pass is used to pass the ball over a defender. Raise the ball over your head with both arms, and throw the ball to another player. The goal is to throw high enough so that the defender cannot reach the ball.

The ball must be held right above the head (left), not in back (right), for an overhead pass. Otherwise, your opponent might try to grab it!

SHOOTING THE BALL

While being tall can help, the key to shooting a basketball is proper form and lots of practice!

The more you practice, the better your shooting will become.

Proper positioning is often the single most important part of the shot.

HOW TO SHOOT A BASKETBALL

1. Keep your eyes on the rim of the basket.

2. Stand with your feet shoulder-width apart and your knees bent.

3. Stagger your feet with your shooting foot in front, pointed in the direction of the basket.

4. Hold the ball in front of you with your shooting hand at the back, and hold your non-shooting hand on the side for balance. This is called your **shot pocket**.

5. Raise the ball upward from the shot pocket, so your elbow is under the ball.

6. Use the power in your legs, core, and arms to jump, then extend your wrist and elbow in a straight line to the basket.

7. Release the ball with a slight backspin just before the top of the your jump, and land in the same spot.

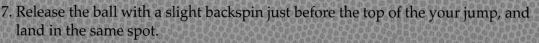

MANY WAYS TO SCORE

Free throws are taken from the free-throw line by players who have been fouled. Three-pointers are made from the three-point line during play. Free throws and three-point shots use the same basic shooting technique. Lay-ups, jump shots, slam dunks, and hook shots use the same technique and combine it with jumping.

FROM LAY-UP TO SLAM DUNK

In a lay-up, the player uses one hand to bounce the ball off the backboard and into the basket. In a jump shot, players shoot the ball while in midair. The hook shot is made with one hand lifting the ball above the player's head with a sweeping motion. In a slam dunk, players lift the ball above the rim and slam it directly into the basket.

Curry plays point guard for Golden State.

SHOOTING DRILL: MASTERING FREE THROWS

Before you can do lay-ups and jump shots, you must master basic shooting. Try starting with the free throw. Stand at the free-throw line and follow the steps for shooting a basket. Keep track and see how many baskets you can make in a row. If you miss one, start again at zero.

SLAM DUNK!

Stephen Curry is one of the best free-throw shooters in the NBA. He makes more than nine out of ten free throws. Most NBA players are successful about seven out of 10 times. Some players only score on half their shots.

REBOUNDING

When a player catches the ball after another player misses a shot, it is called a rebound. The team that wins the rebound gets possession of the ball. **Offensive rebounds** happen when the shooter or the shooter's teammate gets the ball, and the team can attempt to shoot again. When a player from the other team gets the ball, it's called a **defensive rebound**. After a defensive rebound, the rebounding team must move the ball down the court. Good rebounding is an important part of winning a basketball game.

The best position for a rebound changes with every shot. The farther a shot is taken from, the farther the ball will rebound off the hoop.

SLAM DUNK!

Wilt Chamberlain was the best rebounder in basketball history. He led the league in rebounds during 11 of his 14 NBA seasons. He made more than 23,000 rebounds in his career. He once had 55 rebounds in a single game!

FIGHTING FOR THE BALL

Rebounding involves two things—good positioning and jumping. Players must position themselves, then time their jump to beat their opponents to the ball. Players use a technique called **boxing out** to stop the other team from getting rebounds. To box out another player, you position yourself between your opponent and the basket. After catching a rebound, hold the ball at chest level with your elbows out. The rebounder can then turn on one foot, look for an open teammate, and pass the ball.

When you capture a rebound, your team gets the ball and another chance to score.

REBOUNDING DRILL

Rebounding helps a team win games, so don't forget to practice. To practice rebounding, bounce the ball off the backboard next to the net. Jump as high as you can, catch the ball in the air, then hold onto the ball with both hands as you land.

PLAYING DEFENSE

Every basketball coach will tell you that defense wins games. Good defense keeps the other team from scoring and wins possession of the ball. Defenders do this by forcing offensive players to pass the ball instead of shooting, and by blocking passes and shots.

DEFENSIVE POSITIONING

In a good defensive position, players bend their knees with their feet facing forward and legs wide apart. A player's arms should be held out to the side, elbows bent, with their hands wide and facing forward. Defenders move with the offensive player. The defender may not block, grab, hold, or push the offensive player. It's important to keep your eye on the player and on the ball. Most defense happens near the basket. But in a **full-court press**, the defending team uses aggressive defense on the entire court, as soon as the other team has the ball.

Defenders must be careful to follow the rules. If they use too much force, the referees can throw them out of the game.

ZONE VERSUS PLAYER-TO-PLAYER

There are two types of defense: **zone** and player-to-player. In player-to-player defense, each player defends a specific player on the other team. In zone defense, each player defends an assigned area of the court, no matter which offensive player is there.

FAVORITE DEFENSES

Player-to-player defense is more aggressive than zone defense, and more common at the higher levels of play, such as in the NBA. Zone defense is more common in international competition, and in college and youth basketball. The best teams are able to use both types of defense.

When guarding a player, you must also keep track of the ball. If you can't see both, adjust your position.

Many coaches in youth basketball use zone defense because it is less tiring, and it helps players learn to communicate and work together.

IT ALL DEPENDS

Which defense is best depends on the opposing team's skills and weaknesses. Zone defense keeps players away from the basket, so it works well against teams that don't shoot well from far away. Player-to-player defense is used when there is a strong offensive player that must be guarded at all times.

GREAT GUARDS

There are two players known as guards on a five-person basketball team. Guards are usually the shortest members of the team, but they also have the best ball-handling skills.

FLOOR GENERAL

The point guard is often the fastest player on the team. Sometimes known as the floor general, the point guard controls the ball and organizes the offense. The most important job of a point guard is to get the ball to the right shooter at the right time. The point guard is often identified as position 1 on court diagrams.

A point guard must concentrate on setting up the best plays for the team as a whole.

SLAM DUNK!

An assist is given to a player who passes the ball to a teammate in a way that leads to a score by field goal. John Stockton, who played for the Utah Jazz, leads the NBA for most career assists with 15,806.

SHOOTING FROM AFAR

The shooting guard is usually taller than the point guard, and might not be as good at ball handling. The shooting guard plays on the perimeter of the court, or outside the key. The main job of the shooting guard is to take shots from the perimeter. So shooting guards must be very good at scoring points from outside the key, or even the three-point line. The shooting guard is identified as position 2 in court diagrams. Shooting guards may also be known as a **wing** because they play on the outside of the court.

A shooting guard usually can make long shots as well as play defense.

DIANA TAURASI

Diana Taurasi is one of the best all-time guards in basketball. She won the WNBA Rookie of the Year Award in 2004, and played for the Phoenix Mercury for 11 seasons. She was named one of the Top 15 players in WNBA history. Taurasi now plays for a professional league in Russia. Taurasi has played point guard and shooting guard. But at 6 feet (1.8 m) tall, she's average height for women players, so sometimes she plays forward while a shorter teammate plays guard.

Diana Taurasi is one of only seven women to win a NCAA championship, a WNBA championship, and an Olympic gold medal.

FANTASTIC FORWARDS

There are two forwards on a five-person basketball team. Forwards are usually the players with the best all-around skills. They are taller than guards, but still fast and agile. Forwards must be strong ball handlers and excellent shooters.

SMALL FORWARDS

The small forward is the all-purpose player who scores points from the perimeter and from inside the key. Small forwards often drive the ball to the basket, and also get rebounds and steal the ball on defense. The small forward is identified as position 3 on the court. Like the shooting guard, the small forward may also be called a wing.

Because small forwards are fast and agile, they often get the job of guarding the other team's best players.

POWER FORWARDS

The power forward is usually larger and taller than the small forward, and often plays under the basket like the center. Power forwards use their size to get rebounds and their speed to move the ball around the court. The power forward is identified as position 4 on the court.

*The power forward plays the **post**.*

HONING YOUR SKILLS

Youth basketball usually takes a simpler approach to player positions. Two wings play outside the key on the sides, two **posts** play near the basket on either side, and one player is in the role of point guard. As players grow and develop their skills they can take on more specific roles on the court.

James holds the NBA playoff record for most games with at least 30 points, 10 rebounds, and 5 assists.

LeBRON JAMES

LeBron James is not only one of the best forwards in basketball, he may be one of the best players of all time. He has played the small forward and power forward positions for the Cleveland Cavaliers and the Miami Heat. James has won the NBA Rookie of the Year award, two NBA championships, four Most Valuable Player Awards, two Finals MVPs, and two Olympic gold medals. He has been selected to 11 NBA All-Star teams. He holds numerous NBA records for regular season games and playoff games.

AMAZING CENTERS

The center is the tallest player on the court and is often known as "the big man." Centers play close to the basket, and use their size and height to score baskets or defend against the other team. When on offense, centers often stand with their back to the basket and catch passes from their teammates. Then they pivot toward the basket to shoot the ball.

A strong center can dominate the area around the basket with rebounding and blocking.

Abdul-Jabbar could even make behind-the-back dunks.

SLAM-DUNK KING

During his freshman year at UCLA in 1966, center Lew Alcindor dominated the college game with his dunk shot. In 1967, the National Collegiate Athletic Association (NCAA) banned slam dunks. The decision was known as the "Alcindor Rule." The master slam dunker, who changed his name to Kareem Abdul-Jabbar, went on to play 20 years in the NBA. After a nine-year ban, the NCAA allowed college players to dunk once more.

JUMPING HIGH

Centers are usually the best at jump shots, hook shots, and slam dunks. Centers also play an important role on defense by blocking shots and getting rebounds. Usually, centers take the jump ball at the start of play because of their size.

The center position is known as position 5.

Yao Ming towered over the court at 7-feet-6 inches (2.29 m) but still moved fast. Yao, who retired in 2011, helped the NBA win new fans in his native China.

LISA LESLIE

Lisa Leslie is one of the best centers in basketball. She played in the WNBA for 11 seasons for the Los Angeles Sparks. She won two WNBA championships and four Olympic gold medals during her career, and played in the WNBA All-Star game eight times. At 6 ft 5 in (1.96 m), Leslie was one of the tallest women on the court. She was the first player to dunk in the WNBA—but she started dunking as a high school player. Leslie was voted one of the Top 15 players in WNBA history. In 2015, she was elected to the Basketball Hall of Fame.

Leslie helped bring fans to the WNBA when it was just getting started.

27

SPORTSMANSHIP

Good sportsmanship in basketball means always following the rules, showing respect to everyone on the court, and congratulating your opponent after the game—win or lose.

SHARE THE BALL

Never criticize teammates for making mistakes. And don't be a ball hog—basketball is a team sport. You should always work together with your teammates rather than trying to do it all by yourself.

SHOW COURTESY

Basketball is a physical game and accidents can happen on the court. When your opponents are knocked down, stop to help them up. And if your actions have injured a player, always apologize. Fouls happen but you should avoid committing them as much as possible.

Being a good sport means showing respect to other players before, during, and after games.

RESPECT OTHERS

Be positive. No one likes sore losers or players that lose their temper. Sportsmanship also includes respecting officials and the decisions they make. Do not argue with referees when you don't agree with a call. You should always respect your coaches and their decisions during games and practices.

Youth coaches teach more than just basketball skills. They make sure their players also learn good sportsmanship.

NUTRITION

Basketball is a high-energy sport—and players need plenty of fuel. Good, healthy foods give players the energy they need for practices and games. But not all foods are good—chips, candy, and sugary drinks may seem to give you a boost of energy, but the effect doesn't last. Stick to whole grains, starchy vegetables, and fruit for energy. Eating **protein** at every meal will help develop your muscles. Protein also helps your body recover after a workout. A healthy post-game snack might include a whole-grain bagel with peanut butter, or a tuna sandwich.

Hydration is also important. Be sure to drink plenty of fluids during practice and games, and continue to drink water afterward to rehydrate.

PLAY LIKE A PRO

Basketball may seem simple, but the skills and strategies are difficult to master. Start by working on your shooting and ball handling. If you can learn to control the ball and develop good shooting form, the rest of the game will come as you get bigger and stronger. Watching the NBA or other professional games can be exciting, but the level of play is so high that it's hard to learn from the players' examples. Instead, try watching local high school games. There are also many good coaching videos online that can show you the basics.

JUST FOR FUN

The best way to learn to play basketball is to get out on the court. A hoop and ball are all you need! You can practice on your own or with friends, but remember that practicing by yourself is very different from team basketball. Look for youth leagues and camps in your area if you would like to learn more about this exciting and fast-paced game.

You can learn a lot from high school and college teams, or even competitive youth leagues in your area.

LEARNING MORE

Check out these books and websites to find out more about the game.

BOOKS

Basketball: From tip-off to slam dunk—the essential guide by Clive Gifford. Kingfisher, 2012

Play Basketball Like a Pro: Key Skills and Tips by Nate LeBoutillier. Sports Illustrated for Kids, 2010

Top 25 Basketball Skills, Tips, and Tricks by John Albert Torres. Enslow Publishers, 2011

WEBSITES

USA Basketball

www.usab.com

USA Basketball is the governing body of basketball in the United States. The association's youth development program provides excellent skill videos and instructions for all basketball fundamentals.

Canada Basketball

www.basketball.ca

Canada Basketball is the governing body of basketball in Canada. It's also home to the Steve Nash Youth Basketball initiative.

GLOSSARY

Note: Some boldfaced words are defined where they appear in the text.

carrying When a player puts their hand under the ball while dribbling

defense The team who defends their basket against the offense

dribbling The controlled bouncing of the basketball

dynamic warmup A series of movements that help warm up the body for activity

floor leader A player (usually the point guard) who is the extension of the coach on the floor and provides leadership for the team

foul When a player makes contact with another player that is against the rules

free throw A basketball shot worth one point that must be made from behind a specific line and is given because of a foul by an opponent

jump ball When both teams get to the ball at the same time, the referee throws the ball in the air and two players jump up to tip it to a teammate

key The area between the basket and the free-throw line also known as the lane

offense The team who has the ball and tries to score points

out-of-bounds When the ball goes outside the border lines of the court

possession Control of the ball—the team with possession is on offense

post The area around the key. The low post is on either side of the basket and the high post is near the free-throw line; can also refer to a player that plays near the basket

protein A substance essential for life found in foods such as meat, milk, eggs, nuts, and beans

rebound Getting the ball after missing a shot at the basket

shot clock A clock that times a team's possession; teams must shoot the ball before the shot clock runs out

shot pocket The position of the ball at the beginning of a basketball shot

traveling Taking more than one or two steps, depending on the starting position, while holding the ball but not dribbling

three-second rule An offensive player may not stand in the key for more than three seconds

violation When a player breaks a rule such as traveling or the three-second rule

wing The area farther away from the key; there is a left wing and a right wing

INDEX

Abdul-Jabbar, Kareem 26
assists 14, 22, 25
ball handling 11, 22, 23, 30
bounce passes 15
centers 7, 25, 26, 27
Chamberlain, Wilt 18
chest passes 14
Curry, Stephen 17
defense 8, 9, 20, 21, 23, 24, 27
dribbling 8, 12, 13
dynamic warmups 10
fouls 9
free throws 6, 9, 17
full-court press 20
hook shots 17, 27
Irving, Kyrie 13
James, LeBron 25

Johnson, Earvin "Magic" 14
jump ball 7, 27
key 6, 8, 14, 16, 23, 24, 25
lay-ups 11, 17
Leslie, Lisa 27
Naismith, James 4
nutrition 29
offense 8, 14, 22, 26
out-of-bounds 8
overhead passes 15
Paralympic Games 5
passing 8, 11, 14
player-to-player defense 21
point guards 13, 17, 22, 23, 25
posts 25
power forwards 25
rebounds 11, 18, 19, 24, 25, 27

referees 7, 8, 9, 20, 29
shootarounds 11
shooting 5, 7, 11, 12, 16, 17, 20
shooting guards 23, 24
shot clocks 8
slam dunks 17, 26, 27
small forwards 24, 25
sportsmanship 28–29
Taurasi, Diana 23
three-point line 6, 8, 17, 23
three-second rule 8
traveling 8, 9
violations 9
Yao, Ming 27
YMCA 4
zone defense 21